Ugh, That's Ugly!

World Book, Inc.
180 North LaSalle Street
Suite 900
Chicago, Illinois 60601
USA

For information about other World Book publications, visit our website at **www.worldbook.com** or call **1-800-WORLDBK (967-5325)**.

Library of Congress Cataloging-in-Publication data has been applied for.
Title: Ugh! Yuck! and Whoa! Ugh, That's Ugly!
ISBN: 978-0-7166-3711-0

Ugh! Yuck! and Whoa!
ISBN: 978-0-7166-3708-0 (set, hc)

Also available as:
ISBN: 978-0-7166-3719-6 (e-book)

1st printing July 2018

Introduction

Nature is filled with some amazing creatures. From ocean bottoms to mountain tops, from hot deserts to freezing tundra, the *Ugh! Yuck! and Whoa!* books highlight the most extreme animals: the grossest, the deadliest, the strangest, and the rudest! This book is all about ugly animals. Some are slimy, some are creepy, and some are downright strange! Most of the time, these ugly **features** help the animal survive in its **habitat.** An animal that we might think of as ugly might be attractive to other animals of the same **species**—beauty is in the eye of the beholder! Read on to learn all about the freakiest **features** on the ugliest animals. This Gross-O-Meter will show each animal's ugly factor!

BLOBFISH

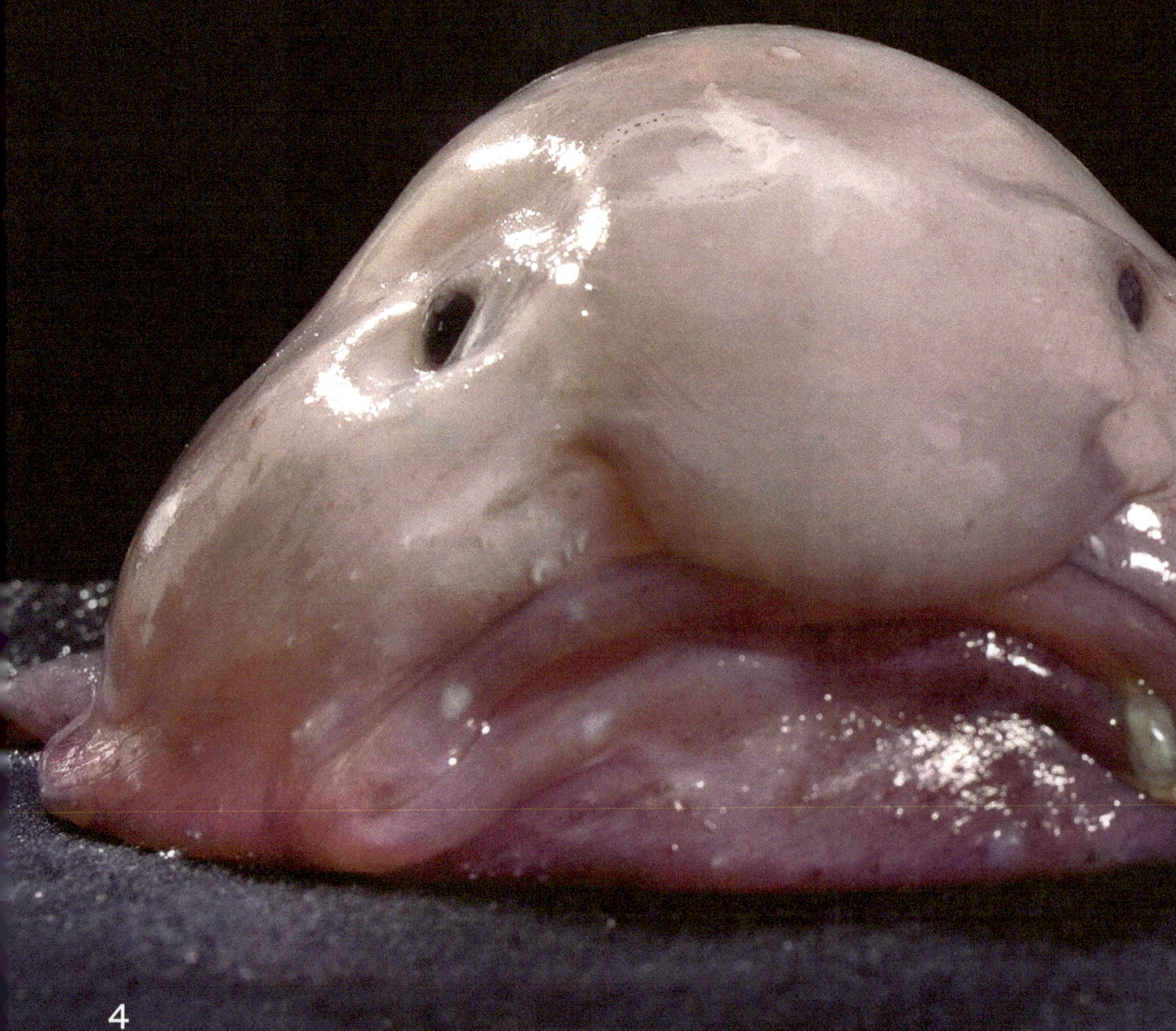

The blobfish lives deep in the ocean.
Its body is gelatinous *(juh LAT uh
nuhs)*. That means it looks and feels
like jelly! The blobfish doesn't swim
very well. Its jellylike flesh helps it float through
the water. The blobfish lives so deep that it can't
have a skeleton of hard bones like most other fish.
They would break under the pressure of the water
above the animal. Instead, the blobfish
has soft bones.

The blobfish looks more like a regular fish when it is in its deep ocean home. But when the blobfish is brought out of the water, it looks like a pile of melting goo!

WRINKLE-FACED BAT

The wrinkle-faced bat isn't the only strange-looking type of bat! The greater bulldog bat is also named for its freaky appearance. Its squished, squat face looks like the face of a bulldog!

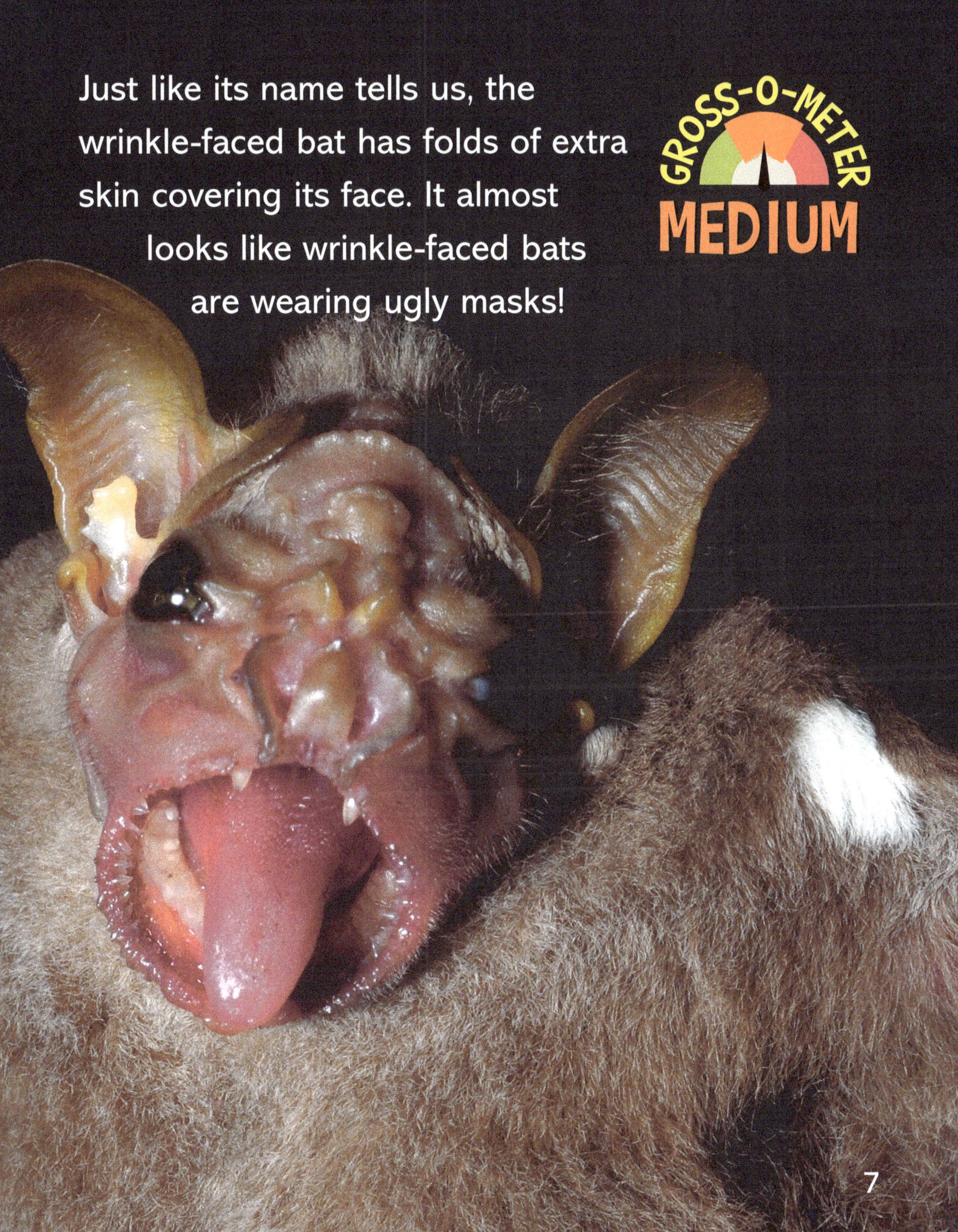

Just like its name tells us, the wrinkle-faced bat has folds of extra skin covering its face. It almost looks like wrinkle-faced bats are wearing ugly masks!

NAKED MOLE-RAT

This little rodent has no hair to cover its pink skin. The naked mole-rat uses its huge front teeth to dig tunnels in the ground.

Naked mole-rats rarely get cancer and can go for up to 18 minutes without oxygen! Naked mole-rats don't get old the way other animals do. They live much longer than scientists first thought they could.

Naked Animals

Naked mole-rats aren't the only animals with no hair. Being hairless is an **adaptation** that helps these animals survive in their **habitats**. Check out some other naked animals!

Mexican hairless dog

Sphynx cats

Hairless rat

Hairless guinea pig

GOBLIN SHARK

The goblin shark has a long, flat snout and a mouth full of sharp, spiky teeth. The snout is the part on the front of an animal's head where the mouth, nose, and jaws are. The goblin shark got its name because its face looks like the face of a creature from European folktales called a goblin.

STAR-NOSED MOLE

Moles are small animals that live mostly underground. The star-nosed mole has a fringe of fleshy tentacles (feelers) around its nose. There isn't any light underground, so moles have tiny eyes and can't see very well. The star-nosed mole's freaky feelers help it find prey as it digs through the ground.

PROBOSCIS MONKEY

A *proboscis (proh BOS ihs)* is a long nose. That's exactly what the proboscis monkey has! This monkey's huge nose hangs over its mouth.

GROSS-O-METER
LOW

Notable Noses

Animal noses come in all shapes and sizes. Some are long, some are oddly shaped, and some are barely there at all!

Snub-nosed monkey

Elephant
Leaf-nosed bat
Saiga
Hammerhead shark

BEARDED PIG

The bearded pig has a long snout covered by hair. Its "beard" of fluffy white hair sits on the top of its long nose.

GROSS-O-METER
LOW

UAKARI

Uakari *(wah KAHR ee)* is a type of South American monkey. The bald-headed uakari are easy to spot by their hairless, bright red faces! Their faces look like red skulls.

GROSS-O-METER
LOW

STARGAZER

Stargazer fish have eyes on top of their head! They bury themselves in the sand and look up toward the sky, giving stargazers their name. Their mouths also face upward so that they can leap from the sand to snatch their prey.

Yuck!

Stargazers are **venomous** (poisonous). They have two spikes that can poison their prey. Some stargazers can even make electric shocks!

BABIRUSA

Babirusas are cousins of pigs. Male babirusas have weird tusks. Tusks are very long, pointed teeth. Babirusa tusks grow from their jaw. They poke through the animal's skin as they grow.

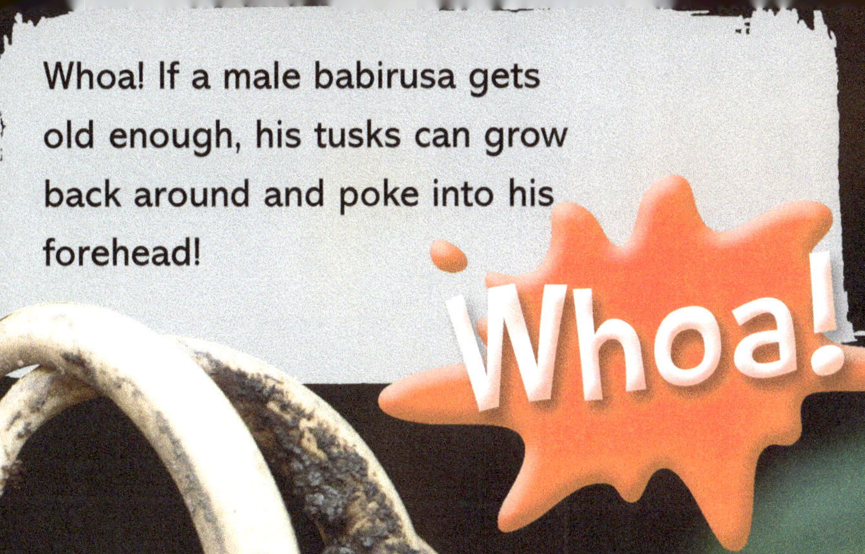

Whoa! If a male babirusa gets old enough, his tusks can grow back around and poke into his forehead!

Whoa!

GROSS-O-METER
MEDIUM

WOLFFISH

Wolffish can grow more than 5 feet (1.5 meters) long and weigh more than 40 pounds (18 kilograms). That's as heavy as a 3-year-old child and as long as a refrigerator is tall!

Wolffish are aggressive ocean fish. (Aggressive—*uh GREHS ihv*—means ready to attack.) They have large, pointed front teeth, which they use to tear apart their food. Their powerful jaws crush the shells of clams, crabs, and other hard-shelled animals they eat. They are named after wolves because of their scary-looking teeth!

PEACOCK
FLOUNDER

Flounders lay sideways on the ocean floor. Both of their eyeballs are on the top side of their head!

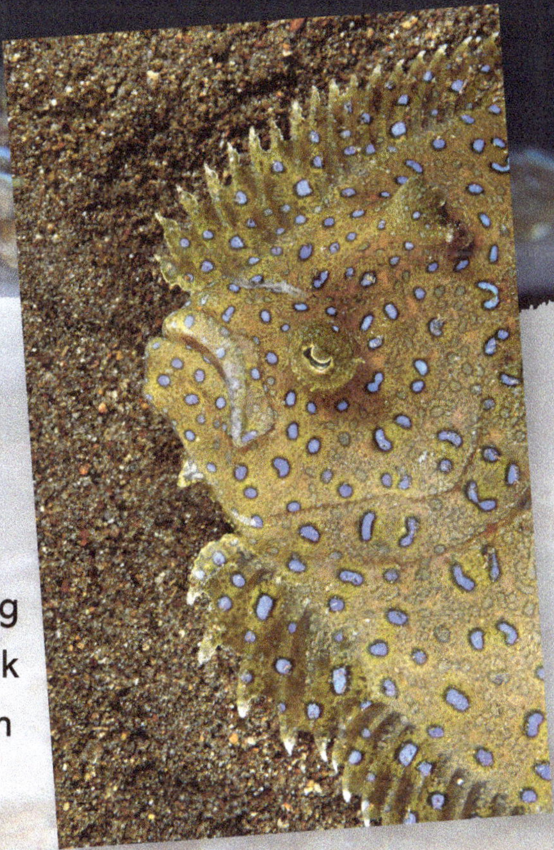

Flounders are great at matching their surroundings. The peacock flounder can change its color in just seconds!

ELEPHANT SEAL

A grown-up male elephant seal can weigh up to 8,800 pounds (4,000 kilograms). That's more than 2 cars, more than 8 grand pianos, and more than 16 pigs!

Elephant seals get their name from their large size and from the male's long nose. The nose looks like an elephant's trunk!

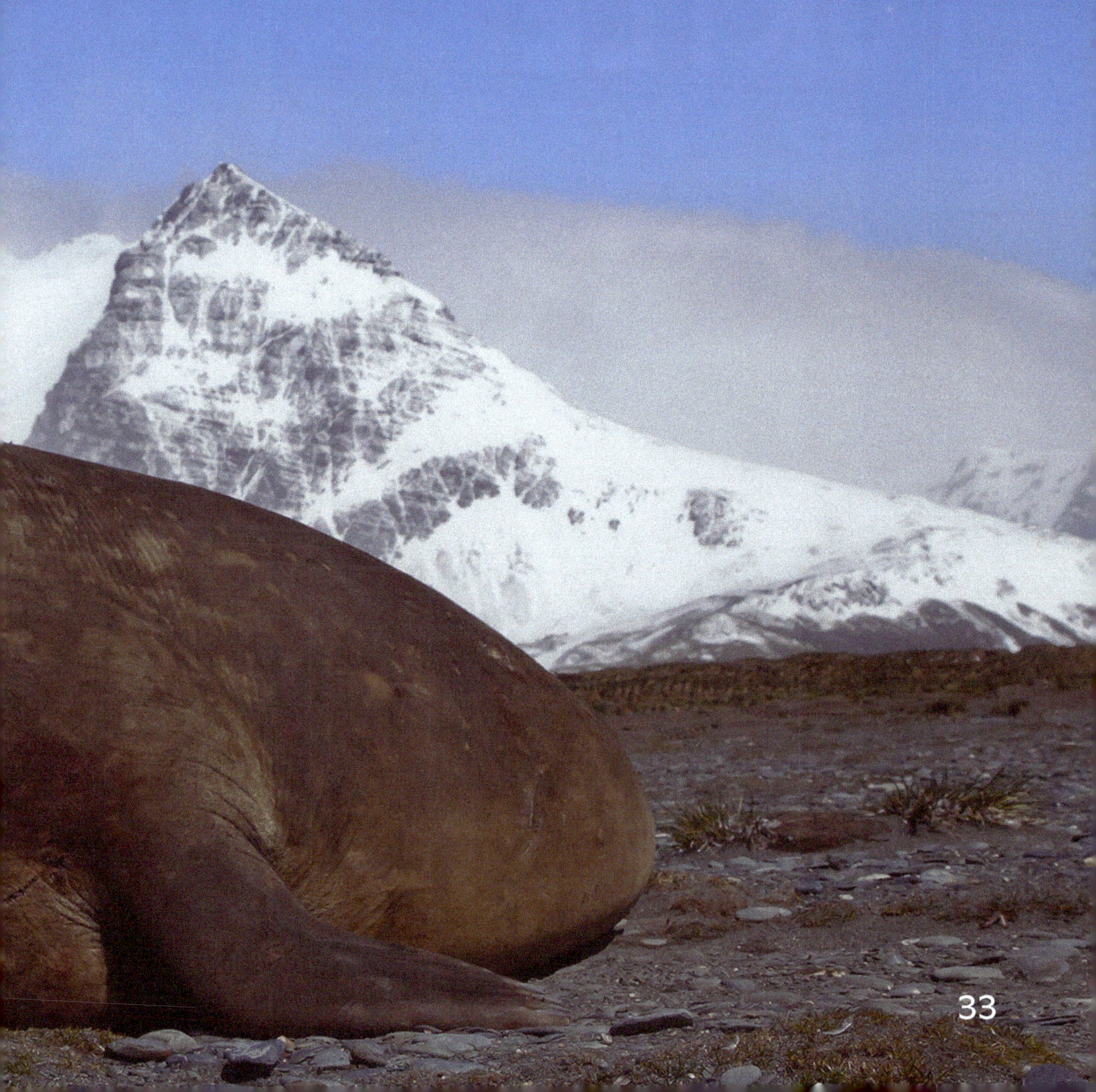

SOFTSHELL TURTLE

These funny-looking turtles have long noses shaped like tubes. Their beaks have fleshy lips. Their shells are soft and leathery, not hard and bumpy like other turtles.

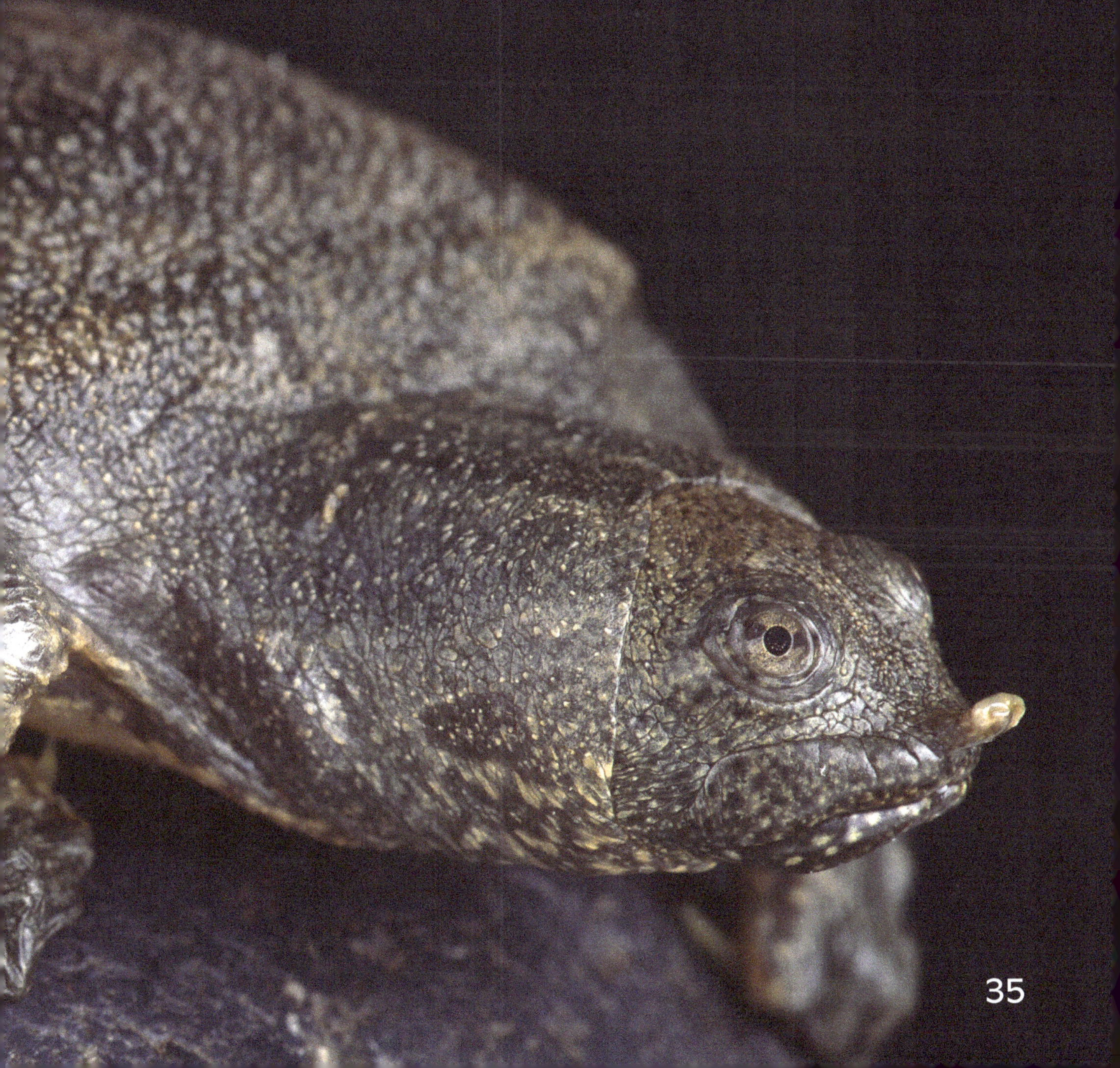

MARABOU STORK

Storks are birds with long legs, strong wings, and a long, pointed beak. The marabou stork is one of the largest storks. It doesn't have feathers on its head or neck. This way, the marabou stork's head and neck do not get covered in blood when it eats other animals.

GROSS-O-METER
MEDIUM

BOBBIT WORM

This type of worm lives in the warm, shallow parts of the world's oceans. It hides in the sand and jumps out to grab any prey that wanders by! The Bobbit worm has such sharp, strong jaws that it sometimes cuts its prey right in half when it attacks.

Ugh!

Bobbit worms are some of the largest worms. They can grow to be more than 12 feet (3.7 meters) long! That's as long as a small car!

CALIFORNIA CONDOR

The California condor is the largest flying land bird in North America. Its wingspan is about 9 feet (3 meters). The California condor has a featherless head and neck. Its wrinkled skin is red-orange beneath its coat of black feathers.

Whoa!

California condors are endangered, which means they are close to dying out. There are only about 400 left in the world. It's important to protect these animals—even if they might be ugly!

MONKFISH

These freaky fish have a broad, flat head. Their mouths reach all the way across their faces! Monkfish have lots of long, sharp teeth.

The fins on the bottom of a monkfish's body can work like feet. Monkfish can push themselves across the ocean floor in a way that looks like walking!

TARSIER

Tarsiers *(TAHR see uhrs)* have huge, round eyes. Each eye is as big as a tarsier's brain! Tarsiers hold onto the trees they climb with their long, skinny fingers and toes.

Glossary

Adaptation

a change in structure, form, or habits to fit different conditions.

Feature

a distinct part or quality.

Habitat

the place where a plant or animal naturally lives and grows.

Species

a group of animals or plants that have certain traits in common and can reproduce (make more animals like themselves) with each other.

Venom

a liquid that an animal makes to stun, injure, or kill another animal through biting or stinging.

Venomous

poisonous; a producer of venom.

Index

Acknowledgments

Cover: © Edwin Giesbers, Nature Picture Library; © Neil Bromhallm, Nature Picture Library

4-5 © Kerryn Parkinson, NORFANZ/Caters News/ZUMA Press; © Kyodo/AP Photo

6-7 © Andrew M. Snyder, Getty Images; © Andrew Snyder, MYN/ Nature Picture Library

8-9 © Neil Bromhall, Nature Picture Library

10-11 © Animal Info/iStockphoto; © Lynn M. Stone, Nature Picture Library; © Les Palenik, Shutterstock; © Life On White/ Getty Images

12-13 © Kelvin Aitken, VWPics/Alamy Images

14-15 © Rod Planck, Science Photo Library

16-17 © Anup Shah, Nature Picture Library

18-19 © Anup Shah, Nature Picture Library; © Florian MÃllers, Nature Picture Library; © Andrew Snyder, MYN/Nature Picture Library; © Paul Johnson, Nature Picture Library; © Davi Fleetham, Nature Picture Library

20-21 © Edwin Giesbers, Nature Picture Library

22-23 © Ingo Arndt, Nature Picture Library

24-25 © Jurgen Freund, Nature Picture Library

26-27 © Nick Garbutt, Nature Picture Library

28-29 © Florian Graner, Nature Picture Library

30-31 © Claudio Contreras, Nature Picture Library; © Brandon Cole, Nature Picture Library

32-33 © Mzphoto.cz/Shutterstock

34-35 © Reptiles4al/Shutterstock

36-37 © Visuals Unlimited/Nature Picture Library

38-39 © Alex Mustard, Nature Picture Library

40-41 © Claudio Contreras, Nature Picture Library

42-43 © Wild Wonders of Europe/Lundgren/Nature Picture Library

44-45 © Tim Laman, Nature Picture Library